Non-Fiction Common Core Readings
Book 3: Discovering America Series

John Adams: Non-Fiction Readings

Interactive Common Core Workbook

By

Elizabeth Chapin-Pinotti

Table of Contents
and Common Core State Standards Alignment

John Adams Facts

Birth Date: October 30, 1735

Birth Place: Braintree, Massachusetts

Died: July 4, 1826

Education: Harvard University
- 1755 undergraduate graduation
- 1758 master's degree

Occupation: Attorney

Remembered For: Federalist views, Alien and Sedition Acts

Offices Held:
- First Vice President
- Second President

Married to: Abigail Adams

Noted Facts:
- Direct descendant of Puritan colonists from the Massachusetts Bay Colony
- At 16 he earned a scholarship to Harvard University
- 1758 admitted to the bar
- 1774 served on the First Continental Congress
- Helped draft the Declaration of Independence
- Was the only Federalist President
- Was the only one of the first five Presidents of the United States not to be a slave owner
- During the Continental Congresses he served on 90 committees, chairing 20 – more than any other person
- He was the first person to live in the White House
- He moved into the White House before it was completed
- He died on the same day, in the same year, as his rival and friend Thomas Jefferson
- He defended the British soldiers who killed Americans at the Boston Massacre because he believed everyone was entitled to be defended in court

Figure 1: Navel Historical Center, Washington, D.C.: A painting of President John Adams (1735-1826), 2nd president of the United States, by Asher B. Durand (1767-1845).

Important Notes:

XYZ Affair: While Adams was president, the French regularly harassed American ships at sea. Adams attempted to stop the attacks by sending ministers to France. The French sent the ministers away and then sent a note asking for a bribe of $250,000 to hold a meeting with them. Adams was afraid war would begin so he asked Congress for an increase in military spending. His opponents, the Democratic-Republicans, would not agree so Adams released the letter asking for the bribe. He replaced the French signatures with the letters XYZ. This changed the Democratic-Republicans minds. Fearing a public outcry after the release of the letters would bring America closer to war, Adams tried one more time to meet with France. The meetings were successful and peace was preserved.

Alien and Sedition Acts: When war with France seemed likely, acts were implemented that limited immigration and free speech, called the **Alien and Sedition Acts, were passed**. These acts eventually were used against opponents of the Federalists leading to arrests and censorship. **Thomas Jefferson and James Madison wrote the Kentucky and Virginia Resolutions in protest.**

Interpreting Primary Sources

Source Documents: The history we study today comes from analyzing the past by way of primary sources. A primary source is a document or a physical object written or created during the time period being studied. Primary source documents include letters, maps, journals, photographs and drawings. Primary sources also include news film footage, autobiographies, poetry, novels, furniture, clothing and buildings. Examples of primary sources include:

- The Declaration of Independence
- The Constitution of the United States
- Plato's Republic
- A Civil War cannon ball

A secondary source analyzes or interprets primary sources. Secondary sources are one or more steps removed from the event being studied. Secondary sources include textbooks, magazine articles, commentaries and interpretations. Examples of secondary sources include:

- Magazine articles
- History textbooks
- A book about the readings of Thomas Jefferson

Rules for Analyzing Source Documents

Time and Place Rule: The closer to the time and place of the historical event, the more reliable a source is deemed. From top to bottom are the most reliable sources:

- Direct traces of the event;
- Accounts of the event by firsthand observers and/or participants created at the time of the event;
- Accounts of the event by firsthand observers and/or participant; created after the event occurred, by firsthand observers and participants;
- Accounts of the event, created after the event occurred, by people who did not participate or witness the event, but who used interviews or evidence from the time of the event.;
- A letter or journal writing when the event occurred by the parties of the event.

Bias Rule: Historians assume that every source is biased. Each piece must be looked at carefully and critically. Everyone has an opinion, so the creator's point of view must be considered.

Questions to Think About When Analyzing Source Documents:

- Who created the source and why?
- Did the recorder have firsthand knowledge of the event? Or, did the recorder report what others saw and heard?
- Was the recorder a neutral party? What is the personal bias?
- Why was the source produced? Was it personal, like a diary, or public, like a report?
- Did the recorder or author have a reason to be dishonest or was he or she trying to persuade someone?
- Was the information recorded during the event, immediately after the event, or after some time had passed? If time had passed, what was the gap?

Asking yourself these questions as you work through primary sources will help you analyze the source and make a determination. It may be easier, and even tempting, to use a textbook or the internet to help you interpret something that you may not completely understand, but a critical part of the learning process is to think for yourself and form your own opinions. Who knows? You may make some stellar historical breakthrough by thinking of something that no one has ever thought before.

Think of studying history and sorting through both primary and secondary sources as a great scavenger hunt where the prize at the end of the hunt is discovering, maybe even for the first time, what life was like in the past and what led up to major events in history!

On this page is a letter Abigail Adams wrote to her husband in March and April 1776. Think about what was going on in 1776 as you read her words and try to put them into historical context.

Before reading the following letter, please note that the exchange of letters between John and Abigail Adams included well over 1,100 items beginning before they were married and extending throughout his political career. A great resource for this correspondence is the Massachusetts Historical Society at www.masshist.org.

Braintree March 31, 1776

I wish you would ever write me a Letter half as long as I write you; and tell me if you may where your Fleet are gone? What sort of Defence Virginia can make against our common Enemy? Whether it is so situated as to make an able Defence? Are not the Gentery Lords and the common people vassals, are they not like the uncivilized Natives Brittain represents us to be? I hope their Riffel Men who have shewen themselves very savage and even Blood thirsty; are not a specimen of the Generality of the people.

I ~~[illegible]~~ am willing to allow the Colony great merrit for having produced a Washington but they have been shamefully duped by a Dunmore.

I have sometimes been ready to think that the passion for Liberty cannot be Eaquelly Strong in the Breasts of those who have been accustomed to deprive their fellow Creatures of theirs. Of this I am certain that it is not founded upon that generous and christian principal of doing to others as we would that others should do unto us.

Do not you want to see Boston; I am fearfull of the small pox, or I should have been in before this time. I got Mr. Crane to go to our House and see what state it was in. I find it has been occupied by one of the Doctors of a Regiment, very dirty, but no other damage has been done to it. The few things which were left in it are all gone. Cranch has the key which he never deliverd up. I have wrote to him for it and am determined to get it cleand as soon as possible and shut it up. I look upon it a new acquisition of property, a property which one month ago I did not value at a single Shilling, and could with pleasure have seen it in flames.

The Town in General is left in a better state than we expected, more oweing to a percipitate flight than any Regard to the inhabitants, tho some individuals discoverd a sense of honour and justice and have left the rent of the Houses in which they were, for the owners and the furniture unhurt, or if damaged sufficent to make it good.

Others have committed abominable Ravages. The Mansion House of your **President** is safe and the furniture unhurt whilst both

the House and Furniture of the **Solisiter General** have fallen a prey to their own merciless party. Surely the very Fiends feel a Reverential awe for Virtue and patriotism, whilst they Detest the paricide and traitor.

I feel very differently at the approach of spring to what I did a month ago. We knew not then whether we could plant or sow with safety, whether when we had toild we could reap the fruits of our own industery, whether we could rest in our own Cottages, or whether we should not be driven from the sea coasts to seek shelter in the wilderness, but now we feel as if we might sit under our own vine and eat the good of the land.

I feel a gaieti de Coar to which before I was a stranger. I think the Sun looks brighter, the Birds sing more melodiously, and Nature puts on a more chearfull countanance. We feel a temporary peace, and the poor fugitives are returning to their deserted habitations.

Tho we felicitate ourselves, we sympathize with those who are trembling least the Lot of Boston should be theirs. But they cannot be in similar circumstances unless pusilanimity and cowardise should take possession of them. They have time and warning given them to see the Evil and shun it. -- I long to hear that you have declared an independency -- and by the way in the new Code of Laws which I suppose it will be necessary for you to make I desire you would

remember the Ladies, and be more generous and favourable to them than your ancestors. Do not put such unlimited power into the hands of the Husbands. Remember all Men would be tyrants if they could. If perticuliar care and attention is not paid to the Laidies we are determined to foment a Rebelion, and will not hold ourselves bound by any Laws in which we have no voice, or Representation.

That your Sex are Naturally Tyrannical is a Truth so thoroughly established as to admit of no dispute, but such of you as wish to be happy willingly give up the harsh title of Master for the more tender and endearing one of Friend. Why then, not put it out of the power of the vicious and the Lawless to use us with cruelty and indignity with impunity. Men of Sense in all Ages abhor those customs which treat us only as the vassals of your Sex. Regard us then as Beings placed by providence under your protection and in immitation of the Supreem Being make use of that power only for our happiness.

April 5

Not having an opportunity of sending this I shall add a few lines more; tho not with a heart so gay. I have been attending the sick chamber of our Neighbour Trot whose affliction I most sensibly feel but cannot discribe, striped of two lovely children in one week. Gorge the Eldest died on wedensday and Billy the youngest on fryday, with the Canker fever, a terible disorder so much like the throat distemper, that it differs but little from it. Betsy Cranch has been very bad, but upon the recovery. Becky Peck they do not expect will live out the day. Many grown persons are now sick with it, in this street 5. It rages much in other Towns. The Mumps too are very frequent. Isaac is now confined with it. Our own little flock are yet well. My Heart trembles with anxiety for them. God preserve them.

I want to hear much oftener from you than I do. March 8 was the last date of any that I have yet had. -- You inquire of whether I am making Salt peter. I have not yet attempted it, but after Soap making believe I shall make the experiment. I find as much as I can do to manufacture cloathing for my family who which would else be Naked. I know of but one person in this part of the Town who has made any, that is Mr. Tertias Bass as he is calld who has got very near an hundred weight which has been found to be very good. I have heard of some others in the other parishes. Mr. Reed of Weymouth has been applied to, to go to Andover to the mills which are now at work, and has gone. I have lately seen a small Manuscrip describing the proportions for the various sorts of powder, such as fit for cannon, small arms and pistols [illegible] . If it would be of any Service your way I will get it transcribed and send it to you. -- Every one of your Friends send their Regards, and all the little ones. **Your Brothers youngest child** lies bad with convulsion fitts. Adieu. I need not say how much I am Your ever faithfull Friend.

(Letter from Abigail Adams to John Adams, 31 March - 5 April 1776 [electronic edition]. *Adams Family Papers: An Electronic Archive.* Massachusetts Historical Society. http://www.masshist.org/digitaladams/)

Primary Source Analysis

1. Type of Document: _____

2. Date of Document: _____ 3. Author of Document: _____

4. Title of the Document: _____

5. Who is the Document's Intended Audience: _____
_____
_____
_____

6. List three things the author said that you think are important:_____
_____
_____
_____

7. Why do you think the document was written:
_____
_____
_____

8. What is the evidence that helps you understand why it was written:
_____
_____
_____

9. List two things the document tells you about life in the United States at the time it was written:
_____
_____
_____

10. Write a question to the author that is left unanswered by the document:
_____
_____
_____

Stamp Act of 1765

Adams joined the patriot cause early on. He vehemently opposed the Stamp Act of 1765 and wrote a response to the act titled "Essay on the Canon and Feudal Law". The essay was published as a series of articles in the *Boston Gazette*. In his essay, Adams argued that the Stamp Act robbed Americans of the basic right to be taxed with their consent and to be tried by a jury of their peers. Two months later, Adams publicly denounced the act in a speech to the Massachusetts governor and his council.

The Stamp Act of 1765 was passed by the British Parliament on March 22, 1765. The Stamp Act required all Americans to pay a tax on every piece of paper they used. Legal documents, ship papers, licenses, documents, newspapers, and even playing cards were taxed. The British claimed the money raised was to pay for defending and protecting the American Frontier; however, Britain was in debt from the Seven Years' War and was using the American colonies as a revenue source.

The actual taxes imposed were small. The issue was rather the precedent set by the law. In the past, taxes on colonists were duties on colonial trade and not specifically to raise money. The Stamp Act, however, was seen by the colonists as a direct attempt to raise money without the approval of the colonial legislatures, or taxation without representation. This was the first internal tax levied directly by the government. Many colonists feared that if this law passed without any opposition, the floodgates would open for more and more taxation in the future.

Think About: Text of The Stamp Act is on the following pages. A major contention of the colonists was taxation without representation and the precedent levying such taxes would set. The United States has come a long way from the days of The Stamp Act; however, some people feel that current State governments in the United States, as well as the Federal Government, levy taxes, duties and fees without the constitutional authority to do so.

Essay Question: The United States of America is a Federal Constitutional Republic not a direct democracy. Under our Federal Constitutional Republic are taxes currently being levied or assigned whereby citizens can legally apply the tenets of taxation without representation?

1. Read The Stamp Act – using the "Text Marking" strategy
2. Complete The Stamp Act Graphic Organizer
3. Construct your essay
4. Have one peer read your essay and please make revisions as necessary
5. Be prepared to support your stand in a Socratic Seminar

Text Marking

Description of Strategy: *Text Marking* is an interactive reading strategy to help you identify and highlight key ideas within the body of a text. There are three main parts to marking a text.

1. **Number the paragraphs:** Number each paragraph or section as you read. For "The Stamp Act" exercise, begin "numbering" the first paragraph with "a" and continue until you reach the numbered acts – which are numbered for you!
2. **Circle Key Terms:** Think about your learning objective. Why are you reading an assigned piece of text? Think about why you are specifically reading "The Stamp Act".

   What is your objective for reading "The Stamp Act"? _____

   _____

   _____

   _____

   _____

   _____

3. **Underline Information:** Be sure to use pencil as you apply your objective to underline important information.

Note: When you are reading a text you cannot mark, create a T-chart to keep track of essential information:

Key Terms	Essential Ideas
• Key words • People • Places • Content vocabulary • Dates • Data	• Author claims • Evidence • Details • Descriptions • Definitions • Fact

Instructions:
- Read the text once through without marking
- Re-read the prompt or objective and read the text again
- Share your ideas with a partner or in a group – asking "Why did you mark?" or "Why didn't you mark?"
- Summarize your markings

The Stamp Act

March 22, 1765

AN ACT for granting and applying certain stamp duties, and other duties, in the British colonies and plantations in America, towards further defraying the expenses of defending, protecting, and securing the same; and for amending such parts of the several acts of parliament relating to the trade and revenues of the said colonies and plantations, as direct the manner of determining and recovering the penalties and forfeitures therein mentioned.

WHEREAS, by an act made in the last session of Parliament several duties were granted, continued, and appropriated toward defraying the expenses of defending, protecting, and securing the British colonies and plantations in America; and whereas it is just and necessary that provision be made for raising a further revenue within your majesty's dominions in America toward defraying the said expenses; we, your majesty's most dutiful and loyal subjects, the Commons of Great Britain, *in Parliament assembled, have therefore resolved to give and grant unto your majesty the several rates and duties hereinafter mentioned; and do humbly beseech your majesty that it may be enacted, and be it enacted by the king's most excellent majesty, by and with the advice and consent of the lords spiritual and temporal, and commons, in this present Parliament assembled, and by the authority of the same, that from and after the first day of November, one thousand seven hundred and sixty five, there shall be raised, levied, collected, and paid unto his majesty, his heirs, and successors, throughout the colonies and plantations in America, which now are, or hereafter may be, under the dominion of his majesty, his heirs and successors:*

> **Quick Write:** What does this say?

1. For every skin or piece of vellum or parchment, or sheet or piece of paper, on which shall be engrossed, written, or printed, any declaration, plea, replication, rejoinder, demurrer or other pleading, or any copy thereof; in any court of law within the British colonies and plantations in America, a stamp duty of *three pence.*

2. For every skin or piece of vellum or parchment, or sheet or piece of paper, on which shall be engrossed, written, or printed, any special bail, and appearance upon such bail in any such court, a stamp duty of *two shillings.*

3. For every skin or piece of vellum or parchment, or sheet or piece of paper, on which may be engrossed, written, or printed, any petition, bill, answer, claim, plea, replication,

rejoinder, demurrer, or other pleading, in any court of chancery or equity within the said colonies and plantations, a stamp duty of *one shilling and six pence.*

4. For every skin or piece of vellum or parchment, or sheet or piece of paper, on which shall be engrossed, written, or printed, *any copy* of any position, bill, answer, claim, plea, replication, rejoinder, demurrer, or other pleading in any such court, a stamp duty of *three pence.*

5. For every skin or piece of vellum or parchment, or sheet or piece of paper, on which shall be engrossed, written, or printed, any monition, libel, answer, allegation, inventory, or renunciation in ecclesiastical matters, in any court of probate court of the ordinary, or other court exercising ecclesiastical jurisdiction within the said colonies and plantations, a stamp duty of *one shilling.*

6. For every skin or piece of vellum or parchment, or sheet or piece of paper, on which shall be engrossed, written, or printed, any copy of any will (other than the probate thereof) monition, libel, answer, allegation, inventory, or renunciation in ecclesiastical matters, in any such court, a stamp duty of *six pence.*

7. For every skin or piece of vellum or parchment, or sheet or piece of paper, on which shall be engrossed, written, or printed, any donation, presentation, collation or institution, of or to any benefice, or any writ or instrument for the like purpose, or any register, entry, testimonial, or certificate of any degree taken in any university, academy, college, or seminary of learning within the said colonies and plantations, a stamp duty of *two pounds.*

8. For every skin or piece of vellum or parchment, or sheet or piece of paper, on which shall be engrossed, written, or printed, any monition, libel, claim, answer, allegation, information, letter of request, execution, renunciation, inventory, or other pleading, in any admiralty court, within the said colonies and plantations, a stamp duty of *one shilling.*

9. For every skin or piece of vellum or parchment, or sheet or piece of paper, on which any copy of any such monition, libel, claim, answer, allegation, information, letter of request, execution, renunciation, inventory, or other pleading shall be engrossed, written, or printed, a stamp duty of *six pence.*

10. For every skin or piece of vellum or parchment, or sheet or piece of paper, on which shall be engrossed, written, or printed, any appeal, writ of error, writ of dower, *ad quod damnum,* certiorari, statute merchant, statute staple, attestation, or certificate, by any officer, or exemplification of any record or proceeding, in any court whatsoever, within the said colonies and plantations (except appeals, writs of error, certiorari attestations, certificates, and exemplifications, for, or relating to the removal of any proceedings from before a single justice of the peace), a stamp duty of *ten shillings.*

11. For every skin or piece of vellum or parchment, or sheet or piece of paper, on which shall be engrossed, written, or printed, any writ of covenant for levying fines, writ of entry for suffering a common recovery, or attachment issuing out of, or returnable into, any court within the said colonies and plantations, a stamp duty of *five shillings.*

12. For every skin or piece of vellum or parchment, or sheet or piece of paper, on which shall be engrossed, written, or printed, any judgment, decree, sentence, or dismission or any record of *nisi prius* or *postea,* in any court within the said colonies and plantations, a stamp duty of *four shillings.*

13. For every skin or piece of vellum or parchment, or sheet or piece of paper, on which

shall be engrossed, written, or printed, any affidavit, common bail, or appearance, interrogatory, deposition, rule, order or warrant of any court, or any *dedimus potestatem, capias subpoena,* summons, compulsory citation, commission, recognizance, or any other writ, process, or mandate, issuing out of, or returnable into, any court, or any office belonging thereto, or any other proceeding therein whatsoever, or any copy thereof, or of any record not herein before charged, within the said colonies and plantations (except warrants relating to criminal matters, and proceedings thereon, or relating thereto), a stamp duty of *one shilling.*

14. For every skin or piece of vellum or parchment, or sheet or piece of paper, on which shall be engrossed, written, or printed, any note or bill of lading, which shall be signed for any kind of goods, wares, or merchandise, to be exported from, or any cocket or clearance granted within the said colonies and plantations, a stamp duty of *four pence.*

15. For every skin or piece of vellum or parchment, or sheet or piece of paper, on which shall be engrossed, written, or printed, letters of mart or commission for private ships of war, within the said colonies and plantations, a stamp duty of *twenty shillings.*

16. For every skin or piece of vellum or parchment, or sheet or piece of paper, on which shall be engrossed, written, or printed, any grant, appointment, or admission of, or to, any public beneficial office or employment, for the space of one year, or any lesser time, of or *above twenty pounds per annum* sterling money, in salary, fees, and perquisites, within the said colonies and plantations (except commissions and appointments of officers of the army, navy, ordnance, or militia, of judges, and of justices of the peace), a stamp duty of *ten shillings.*

17. For every skin or piece of vellum or parchment, or sheet or piece of paper, on which any grant, of any liberty, privilege, or franchise, under the seal or sign manual of any governor, proprietor, or public officer, alone, or in conjunction with any other person or persons, or with any council, or any council and assembly, or any exemplification of the same, shall be engrossed, written, or printed, within the said colonies and plantations, a stamp duty of *six pounds.*

18. For every skin or piece of vellum or parchment, or sheet or piece of paper, on which shall be engrossed, written, or printed, any license for retailing of spirituous liquors, to be granted to any person who shall take out the same, within the said colonies and plantations, a stamp duty of *twenty shillings.*

19. For every skin or piece of vellum or parchment, or sheet or piece of paper, on which shall be engrossed, written, or printed, any license for retailing of wine, to be granted to any person who shall not take out a license for retailing of spirituous liquors, within the said colonies and plantations, a stamp duty of *four pounds.*

20. For every skin or piece of vellum or parchment, or sheet or piece of paper, on which shall be engrossed, written, or printed, any license for retailing of wine, to be granted to any person who shall take out a license for retailing of spirituous liquors, within the said colonies and plantations, a stamp duty of *three pounds.*

21. For every skin or piece of vellum or parchment, or sheet or piece of paper, on which shall be engrossed, written, or printed, any probate of will, letters of administration, or of guardianship for any estate above the value of twenty pounds sterling money, within the British colonies and plantations upon the continent of America, the islands belonging thereto and the Bermuda and Bahama islands, a stamp duty of *five shillings.*

22. For every skin or piece of vellum or parchment, or sheet or piece of paper, on which

shall be engrossed, written, or printed, any such probate, letters of administration or of guardianship, within all other parts of the British dominions in America, a stamp duty of *ten shillings.*

23. For every skin or piece of vellum or parchment, or sheet or piece of paper, on which shall be engrossed, written, or printed, any bond for securing the payment of any sum of money, not exceeding the sum of ten pounds sterling money within the British colonies and plantations upon the continent of America, the islands belonging thereto, and the Bermuda and Bahama islands, a stamp duty of *six pence.*

24. For every skin or piece of vellum or parchment, or sheet or piece of paper, on which shall be engrossed, written, or printed, any bond for securing the payment of any sum of money above ten pounds, and not exceeding twenty pounds sterling money, within such colonies, plantations, and islands a stamp duty of *one shilling.*

25. For every skin or piece of vellum or parchment, or sheet or piece of paper, on which shall be engrossed, written, or printed, any bond for securing the payment of any sum of money above twenty pounds, arid not exceeding forty pounds sterling money, within such colonies, plantations, and islands, a stamp duty of *one shilling and six pence.*

26. For every skin or piece of vellum or parchment, or sheet or piece of paper, on which shall be engrossed, written, or printed, any order or warrant for surveying or setting out any quantity of land, not exceeding one hundred acres, issued by any governor, proprietor, or any public officer, alone, or in conjunction with any other person or persons, or with any council, or any council and assembly, within the British colonies and plantations in America, a stamp duty of *six pence.*

27. For every skin or piece of vellum or parchment, or sheet or piece of paper, on which shall be engrossed, written, or printed, any such order or warrant for surveying or setting out any quantity of land above one hundred and not exceeding two hundred acres, within the said colonies and plantations, a stamp duty of *one shilling.*

28. For every skin or piece of vellum or parchment, or sheet or piece of paper, on which shall be engrossed, written, or printed, any such order or warrant for surveying or setting out any quantity of land above two hundred, and not exceeding three hundred and twenty acres, and in proportion for every such order or warrant for surveying or setting out every other three hundred and twenty acres, within the said colonies and plantations, a stamp duty of *one shilling and six pence.*

29. For every skin or piece of vellum or parchment, or sheet or piece of paper, on which shall be engrossed, written, or printed, any original grant, or any deed, mesne conveyance, or other instrument whatsoever, by which any quantity of land, not exceeding one hundred acres, shall be granted, conveyed, or assigned, within the British colonies and plantations upon the continent of America, the islands belonging thereto, and the Bermuda and Bahama islands (except leases for any term not exceeding the term of twenty one years), a stamp duty of *one shilling and six pence.*

30. For every skin or piece of vellum or parchment, or sheet or piece of paper, on which shall be engrossed, written, or printed, any such original grant, or any such deed, mesne conveyance, or other instrument whatsoever, by which any quantify of land above one hundred, and not exceeding two hundred acres, shall be granted, conveyed, or assigned, within such colonies, plantations, and islands, a stamp duty of *two shillings.*

31. For every skin or piece of vellum or parchment, or sheet or piece of paper, on which shall be engrossed, written, or printed, any such original grant, or any such deed,

mesne conveyance, or other instrument whatsoever, by which any quantity of land above two hundred, and not exceeding three hundred and twenty acres, shall be granted, conveyed, or assigned, and in proportion for every such grant, deed, mesne conveyance, or other instrument, granting, conveying, or assigning, every other three hundred and twenty acres, within such colonies, plantations, and islands, a stamp duty of *two shillings and six pence.*

32. For every skin or piece of vellum or parchment, or sheet or piece of paper, on which shall be engrossed, written, or printed, any such original grant, or any such deed, mesne conveyance, or other instrument whatsoever, by which any quantity of land, not exceeding one hundred acres, stall be granted, conveyed, or assigned, within all other parts of the British dominions in America, a stamp duty of *three shillings.*

33. For every skin or piece of vellum or parchment, or sheet or piece of paper, on which shall be engrossed, written, or printed, any such original grant, or any such deed, mesne conveyance, or other instrument whatsoever, by which any quantity of land above one hundred, and not exceeding two hundred acres, shall be granted, conveyed, or assigned, within the same parts of the said dominions, a stamp duty of *four shillings.*

34. For every skin or piece of vellum or parchment, or sheet or piece of paper, on which shall be engrossed, written, or printed, any such original grant, or any such deed, mesne conveyance, or other instrument whatsoever, by which any quantity of land above two hundred, and not exceeding three hundred twenty acres, shall he granted, conveyed, or assigned, and in proportion for every such grant, deed, mesne conveyance, or other instrument, granting, conveying, or assigning every other three hundred and twenty acres, within the same parts of the said dominions, a stamp duty of *five shillings.*

35. For every skin or piece of vellum or parchment, or sheet or piece of paper, on which shall be engrossed, written, or printed, any grant, appointment, or admission, of or to any beneficial office or employment, not herein before charged, above the value of twenty pounds *per annum* sterling money in salary, fees, and perquisites, or any exemplification of the same, within the British colonies and plantations upon the continent of America, the islands belonging thereto, and the Bermuda and Bahama islands (except commissions of officers of the army, navy, ordnance, or militia, and of justices of the pence), a stamp duty of *four pounds.*

36. For every skin or piece of vellum or parchment, or sheet or piece of paper, on which shall be engrossed, written, or printed, any such grant, appointment, or admission, of or to any such public beneficial office or employments or any exemplification of the same, within all other parts of the British dominions in America, a stamp duty of *six pounds.*

37. For every skin or piece of vellum or parchment, or sheet or piece of paper, on which shall be engrossed, written, or printed, any indenture, lease, conveyance, contract, stipulation, bill of sale, charter party, protest, articles of apprenticeship or covenant (except for the hire of servants not apprentices, and also except such other matters as herein before charged) within the British colonies and plantations in America, a stamp duty of *two shillings and six pence.*

38. For every skin or piece of vellum or parchment, or sheet or piece of paper, on which any warrant or order for auditing any public accounts, beneficial warrant, order grant, or certificate, under any public seal, or under the send or sign manual of any governor, proprietor, or public officer, alone, or in conjunction with any person or persons, or with any council, or any council and assembly, not herein before charged, or any passport or

let pass, surrender of office, or policy of assurance, shall be engrossed, written, or printed, within the said colonies and plantations (except warrants or orders for the service of the army, navy, ordnance, or militia, and grants of offices under twenty pounds *per annum*, in salary, fees, and perquisites), a stamp duty of *five shillings.*

39. For every skin or piece of vellum or parchment, or sheet or piece of paper, on which shall be engrossed, written or printed, any notarial net, bond, deed, letter of attorney, procuration, mortgage, release, or other obligatory instrument, not herein before charged, within the said colonies and plantations, a stamp duty of *two shillings and three pence.*

40. For every skin or piece of vellum or parchment, or sheet or piece of paper, on which shall be engrossed, written, or printed, any register, entry, or enrollment of any grant, deed or other instrument whatsoever, herein before charged, within the said colonies and plantations, a stamp duty of *three pence.*

41. For every skin or piece of vellum or parchment, or sheet or piece of paper, on which shall be engrossed, written, or printed, any register, entry, or enrollment of any grant, deed, or other instrument whatsoever, not herein before charged, within the said colonies and plantations, a stamp duty of *two shillings.*

42. And for and upon every pack of playing cards, and all dice, which shall be sold or used within the said colonies and plantations, the several stamp duties following (that is to say):

43. For every pack of such cards, *one shilling.*

44. And for every pair of such dice, *ten shillings.*

45. And for and every paper called a *pamphlet*, and upon every newspaper, containing public news or occurrences, which shall be printed, dispersed, and made public, within any of the said colonies and plantations, and for and upon such advertisements as are hereinafter mentioned, the respective duties following (that is to say):

46. For every such pamphlet and paper contained in a half sheet, or any lesser piece of paper, which shall be so printed, a stamp duty of *one half penny* for every printed copy thereof.

47. For every such pamphlet and paper (being larger than half a sheet, and not exceeding one whole sheet), which shall be printed, a stamp duty of *one penny* for every printed copy thereof.

48. For every pamphlet and paper, being larger than one whole sheet, and not exceeding six sheets in octavo, or in a lesser page, or not exceeding twelve sheets in quarto, or twenty sheets in folio, which shall be so printed, a duty after the rate of *one shilling* for every sheet of any kind of paper which shall be contained in one printed copy thereof.

49. For every advertisement to be contained in any gazette newspaper, or other paper, or any pamphlet which shall be so printed, a duty of *two shillings.*

50. For every *almanac,* or calendar, for any one particular year, or for any time less than a year, which shall be written or printed on one side only of any one sheet, skin, or piece of paper, parchment, or vellum, within the said colonies and plantations, a stamp duty of *two pence.*

51. For every other almanac or calendar, for any one particular year, which shall be written or printed within the said colonies and plantations, a stamp duty of *four pence.*

52. And for every almanac or calendar, written or printed in the said colonies and plantations, to serve for several years, duties to the same amount respectively shall be paid for every such year.

53. For every skin or piece of vellum or parchment, or sheet or piece of paper, on which any instrument, proceeding, or other matter or thing aforesaid, shall be engrossed, written, or printed, within the said colonies and plantations, in any other than the English language, a stamp duty of double the amount of the respective duties before charged thereon.

54. And there shall be also paid, in the said colonies and plantations, a duty of six pence for every twenty shillings, in any sum not exceeding fifty pounds sterling money, which shall be given, paid, contracted, or agreed for, with, or in relation to, any clerk or apprentice, which shall be put or placed to or with any master or mistress, to learn any profession, trade, or employment.

II

And also a duty of one shilling for every twenty shillings, in any sum exceeding fifty pounds, which shall be given, paid, contracted, or agreed for, with, or in relation to, any such clerk or apprentice...

V

And be it further enacted ..., That all books and pamphlets serving chiefly for the purpose of an almanack, by whatsoever name or names intituled or described, are and shall be charged with the duty imposed by this act on almanacks, but not with any of the duties charged by this act on pamphlets, or other printed papers ...

VI

Provided always, that this act shall not extend to charge any bills of exchange, accompts, bills of parcels, bills of fees, or any bills or notes not sealed for payment of money at sight, or upon demand, or at the end of certain days of payment....

XII

And be it further enacted ..., That the said several duties shall be under the management of the commissioners, for the time being, of the duties charged on stamped vellum, parchment, and paper, in Great Britain: and the said commissioners are hereby impowered and required to employ such officers under them, for that purpose, as they shall think proper....

XVI

And be it further enacted... That no matter or thing whatsoever, by this act charged with the payment of a duty, shall be pleaded or given in evidence, or admitted in any court within the said colonies and plantations, to be good, useful, or available in law or equity, unless the same shall be marked or stamped, in pursuance of this act, with the respective duty hereby charged thereon, or with an higher duty....

LIV

And be it further enacted ... That all the monies which shall arise by the several rates and duties hereby granted (except the necessary charges of raising, collecting, recovering, answering, paying, and accounting for the same and the necessary charges from time to time incurred in relation to this act, and the execution thereof) shall be paid into the receipt of his Majesty's exchequer, and shall be entered separate and apart from all other monies, and shall be there reserved to be from time to time disposed of by parliament, towards further defraying the necessary expenses of defending, protecting, and securing, the said colonies and plantations....

LVII

... offenses committed against any other act or acts of Parliament relating to the trade or revenues of the said colonies or plantations; shall and may be prosecuted, sued for, and recovered, in any court of record, or in any court of admiralty, in the respective colony or plantation where the offense shall be committed, or in any court of vice admiralty appointed or to be appointed, and which shall have jurisdiction within such colony, plantation, or place, (which courts of admiralty or vice admiralty are hereby respectively authorized and required to proceed, hear, and determine the same) at the election of the informer or prosecutor.....

Essay Question: The United States of America is a Federal Constitutional Republic not a direct democracy. Under our Federal Constitutional Republic are taxes being levied or assigned whereby citizens can legally apply the tenets of taxation without representation?

Summary of "Text Marking" Notes: _____

_____

_____

_____

_____

_____

_____

_____

_____

_____

_____

_____

_____

_____

_____

_____

_____

_____

Critical Thinking Map – The Stamp Act Graphic Organizer

Who is the author? What are his or her professional experiences?

Who is the intended audience?

Author's Central Claim? What argument is being made?

Context: What was happening politically, socially and economically during the time the text was written?

What is the Key Evidence?

What is the author's motivation? What motivated the author to write this? What is the author responding to?

Before You Finish Your Essay

Use the Internet to research the following:

What is a Federal Constitutional Republic?

_____

_____

_____

_____

_____

_____

_____

_____

_____

_____

_____

_____

_____

_____

_____

_____

_____

_____

What is the tax authority of our Federal Constitutional Republic?

_____

_____

_____

_____

_____

_____

_____

_____

_____

_____

_____

_____

_____

_____

_____

Do you think any taxes levied in the United States or in your State are currently being levied that could be considered *taxation without representation*? (Remember to think about HOW we are represented.)

_____

_____

_____

_____

If yes, please list examples and support your assertion. If no, list differences between taxes levied without representations and those levied with representation.

_____

_____

_____

_____

_____

_____

_____

_____

_____

_____

_____

_____

_____

_____

_____

_____

_____

_____

Secondary Source Analysis

From: <u>A COMPILATION OF THE MESSAGES</u>

<u>AND PAPERS OF THE PRESIDENTS</u>

BY JAMES D. RICHARDSON

March 4, 1797, to March 4, 1801

John Adams

John Adams was born on October 19 (old style), 1735, near Boston, Mass., in the portion of the town of Braintree which has since been incorporated as Quincy. He was fourth in descent from Henry Adams, who fled from persecution in Devonshire, England, and settled in Massachusetts about 1630. Another of his ancestors was John Adams, a founder of the Plymouth Colony in 1620. Entered Harvard College in 1751, and graduated therefrom four years later. Studied the law and taught school at Worcester; was admitted to the bar of Suffolk County in 1758. In 1768 removed to Boston, where he won distinction at the bar. In 1764 married Abigail Smith, whose father was Rev. William Smith and whose grandfather was Colonel Quincy. In 1770 was chosen a representative from Boston in the legislature of Massachusetts. In 1774 was a member of the Continental Congress, and in 1776 was the adviser and great supporter of the Declaration of Independence. The same year was a deputy to treat with Lord Howe for the pacification of the Colonies. He declined the offer of chief justice of Massachusetts. In December, 1777, was appointed a commissioner to France, and returned home in the summer of 1779. He was then chosen a member of the Massachusetts convention for framing a State constitution. On September 29, 1779, was appointed by Congress minister plenipotentiary to negotiate a peace treaty with Great Britain. In 1781 was a commissioner to conclude treaties of peace with European powers. In 1783 negotiated with others a commercial treaty with Great Britain. Was one of the commissioners to sign the provisional treaty of peace with that nation November 30, 1782, and the definite treaty September 3, 1783. In 1784 remained in Holland, and in 1785 was by Congress appointed minister of the United States at the Court of Great Britain. He returned to his home in June, 1788. Was chosen Vice-President on the ticket with Washington, and on the assembling of the Senate took his seat as President of that body, at New York in April, 1789. Was reelected Vice-President in 1792. On the retirement of Washington in 1796 he was elected President, and was inaugurated March 4, 1797. He retired March 4, 1801, to his home at Quincy, Mass. In 1816 was chosen to head the list of Presidential electors of his party in the State. Was a member of the State convention to revise the constitution of Massachusetts; was unanimously elected president of that convention, but declined it on account of his age. His wife died in 1818. On July 4, 1826, he died, and was buried at Quincy.

Assignment: Secondary Source Analysis

Secondary Sources: Secondary sources offer analysis of primary sources, with varying reliability and internal biases. Some secondary sources summarize primary sources, while, others pose arguments in attempts to persuade or influence readers.

Questions:

1. Describe the differences between a primary source document and a secondary source document.

_____

_____

_____

2. Who created the source? Does he or she have the appropriate education, background or practical experience to translate or analyze the source?

_____

_____

3. Who is the publisher or what is the domain name? (For example: .edu would be more reliable that .blogspot)

_____

_____

4. Who is the target audience? _____

5. What works are referenced? _____

6. How logical and feasible are the facts and interpretations?

_____

_____

_____

7. Are facts and opinions clearly identified?

_____

_____

_____

8. Why were the secondary sources created?

_____

_____

_____

Primary Source: INAUGURAL ADDRESS IN THE CITY OF PHILADELPHIA

SATURDAY, MARCH 4, 1797

As you read think about: Based solely on the Inaugural Address of John Adams, summary your opinion of President Adams' political views.

When it was first perceived, in early times, that no middle course for America remained between unlimited submission to a foreign legislature and a total independence of its claims, men of reflection were less apprehensive of danger from the formidable power of fleets and armies they must determine to resist than from those contests and dissensions which would certainly arise concerning the forms of government to be instituted over the whole and over the parts of this extensive country. Relying, however, on the purity of their intentions, the justice of their cause, and the integrity and intelligence of the people, under an overruling Providence which had so signally protected this country from the first, the representatives of this nation, then consisting of little more than half its present number, not only broke to pieces the chains which were forging and the rod of iron that was lifted up, but frankly cut asunder the ties which had bound them, and launched into an ocean of uncertainty.

The zeal and ardor of the people during the Revolutionary war, supplying the place of government, commanded a degree of order sufficient at least for the temporary preservation of society. The Confederation which was early felt to be necessary was prepared from the models of the Batavian and Helvetic confederacies, the only examples which remain with any detail and precision in history, and certainly the only ones which the people at large had ever considered. But reflecting on the striking difference in so many particulars between this country and those where a courier may go from the seat of government to the frontier in a single day, it was then certainly foreseen by some who assisted in Congress at the formation of it that it could not be durable.

Negligence of its regulations, inattention to its recommendations, if not disobedience to its authority, not only in individuals but in States, soon appeared with their melancholy consequences-- universal languor, jealousies and rivalries of States, decline of navigation and commerce, discouragement of necessary manufactures, universal fall in the value of lands and their produce, contempt of public and private faith, loss of consideration and credit with foreign nations, and at length in discontents, animosities, combinations, partial conventions, and insurrection, threatening some great national calamity.

In this dangerous crisis the people of America were not abandoned by their usual good sense, presence of mind, resolution, or integrity. Measures were pursued to concert a plan to form a more perfect union, establish justice, insure domestic tranquillity, provide for the common defense, promote the general welfare, and secure the blessings of liberty. The public disquisitions, discussions, and deliberations issued in the present happy Constitution of Government.

Employed in the service of my country abroad during the whole course of these transactions, I first saw the Constitution of the United States in a foreign country. Irritated by no literary altercation, animated by no public debate, heated by no party animosity, I read it with great satisfaction, as the result of good heads prompted by good hearts, as an experiment better adapted to the genius, character, situation, and relations of this nation and country than any which had ever been proposed or suggested. In its general principles and great outlines it was conformable to such a system of government as I had ever most esteemed, and in some States, my own native State in particular, had contributed to establish. Claiming a right of suffrage, in common with my fellow-citizens, in the adoption or rejection of a constitution which was to rule me and my posterity, as well as them and theirs, I did not hesitate to express my approbation of it on all occasions, in public and in private. It was not then, nor has been since, any objection to it in my mind that the Executive and Senate were not more permanent. Nor have I ever entertained a thought of promoting any alteration in it but such as the people themselves, in the course of their experience, should see and feel to be necessary or expedient, and by their representatives in Congress and the State legislatures, according to the Constitution itself, adopt and ordain.

Returning to the bosom of my country after a painful separation from it for ten years, I had the honor to be elected to a station under the new order of things, and I have repeatedly laid myself under the most serious obligations to support the Constitution. The operation of it has equaled the most sanguine expectations of its friends, and from an habitual attention to it, satisfaction in its administration, and delight in its effects upon the peace, order, prosperity, and happiness of the nation I have acquired an habitual attachment to it and veneration for it.

What other form of government, indeed, can so well deserve our esteem and love?

There may be little solidity in an ancient idea that congregations of men into cities and nations are the most pleasing objects in the sight of superior intelligences, but this is very certain, that to a benevolent human mind there can be no spectacle presented by any nation more pleasing, more noble, majestic, or august, than an assembly like that which has so often been seen in this and the other Chamber of Congress, of a Government in which the Executive authority, as well as that of all the branches of the Legislature, are exercised by citizens selected at regular periods by their neighbors to make and execute laws for the general good. Can anything essential, anything more than mere ornament and decoration, be added to this by robes and diamonds? Can authority be more amiable and respectable when it descends from accidents or institutions established in remote antiquity than when it springs fresh from the hearts and judgments of an honest and enlightened people? For it is the people only that are represented. It is their power and majesty that is reflected, and only for their good, in every legitimate government, under whatever form it may appear. The existence of such a government as ours for any length of time is a full proof of a general dissemination of knowledge and virtue throughout the whole body of the people. And what object or consideration more pleasing than this can be presented to the human mind? If national pride is ever justifiable or excusable it is when it springs, not from power or riches, grandeur or glory, but from conviction of national innocence, information, and benevolence.

In the midst of these pleasing ideas we should be unfaithful to ourselves if we should ever lose sight of the danger to our liberties if anything partial or extraneous should infect the purity of our free, fair, virtuous, and independent elections. If an election is to be determined by a majority of a single vote, and that can be procured by a party through artifice or corruption, the Government may be the choice of a party for its own ends, not of the nation for the national good. If that solitary suffrage can be obtained by foreign nations by flattery or menaces, by fraud or violence, by terror, intrigue, or venality, the Government may not be the choice of the American people, but of foreign nations. It may be foreign nations who govern us, and not we, the people, who govern ourselves; and candid men will acknowledge that in such cases choice would have little advantage to boast of over lot or chance.

Such is the amiable and interesting system of government (and such are some of the abuses to which it may be exposed) which the people of America have exhibited to the admiration and anxiety of the wise and virtuous of all nations for eight years under the administration of a citizen who, by a long course of great actions, regulated by prudence, justice, temperance, and fortitude, conducting a people inspired with the same virtues and animated with the same ardent patriotism and love of liberty to independence and peace, to increasing wealth and unexampled prosperity, has merited the gratitude of his fellow-citizens, commanded the highest praises of foreign nations, and secured immortal glory with posterity.

In that retirement which is his voluntary choice may he long live to enjoy the delicious recollection of his services, the gratitude of mankind, the happy fruits of them to himself and the world, which are daily increasing, and that splendid prospect of the future fortunes of this country which is opening from year to year. His name may be still a rampart, and the knowledge that he lives a bulwark, against all open or secret enemies of his country's peace. This example has been recommended to the imitation of his successors by both Houses of Congress and by the voice of the legislatures and the people throughout the nation.

On this subject it might become me better to be silent or to speak with diffidence; but as something may be expected, the occasion, I hope, will be admitted as an apology if I venture to say that if a preference, upon principle, of a free republican government, formed upon long and serious reflection, after a diligent and impartial inquiry after truth; if an attachment to the Constitution of the United States, and a conscientious determination to support it until it shall be altered by the judgments and wishes of the people, expressed in the mode prescribed in it; if a respectful attention to the constitutions of the individual States and a constant caution and delicacy toward the State governments; if an equal and impartial regard to the rights, interest, honor, and happiness of all the States in the Union, without preference or regard to a northern or southern, an eastern or western, position, their various political opinions on unessential points or their personal attachments; if a love of virtuous men of all parties and denominations; if a love of science and letters and a wish to patronize every rational effort to encourage schools, colleges, universities, academies, and every institution for propagating knowledge, virtue, and religion among all classes of the people, not only for their benign influence on the happiness of life in all its stages and classes, and of society in all its forms, but as the only means of preserving our Constitution from its natural enemies, the spirit of sophistry, the spirit of party, the spirit of intrigue, the profligacy of corruption, and the pestilence of foreign influence, which is the angel of destruction to elective governments; if a love of equal laws, of justice, and humanity in the interior administration; if an inclination to improve agriculture, commerce, and manufacturers for necessity, convenience, and

Figure 3: National Portrait Gallery. Smithsonian Institute by John Trumbull. Oil on canvas.

defense; if a spirit of equity and humanity toward the aboriginal nations of America, and a disposition to meliorate their condition by inclining them to be more friendly to us, and our citizens to be more friendly to them; if an inflexible determination to maintain peace and inviolable faith with all nations, and that system of neutrality and impartiality among the belligerent powers of Europe which has been adopted by this Government and so solemnly sanctioned by both Houses of Congress and applauded by the legislatures of the States and the public opinion, until it shall be otherwise ordained by Congress; if a personal esteem for the French nation, formed in a residence of seven years chiefly among them, and a sincere desire to preserve the friendship which has been so much for the honor and interest of both nations; if, while the conscious honor and integrity of the people of America and the internal sentiment of their own power and energies must be preserved, an earnest endeavor to investigate every just cause and remove every colorable pretense of complaint; if an intention to pursue by amicable negotiation a reparation for the injuries that have been committed on the commerce of our fellow-citizens by whatever nation, and if success can not be obtained, to lay the facts before the Legislature, that they may consider what further measures the honor and interest of the Government and its constituents demand; if a resolution to do justice as far as may depend upon me, at all times and to all nations, and maintain peace, friendship, and benevolence with all the world; if an unshaken confidence in the honor, spirit, and resources of the American people, on which I have so often hazarded my all and never been deceived; if elevated ideas of the high destinies of this country and of my own duties toward it, founded on a knowledge of the moral principles and intellectual improvements of the people deeply engraven on my mind in early life, and not obscured but exalted by experience and age; and, with humble reverence, I feel it to be my duty to add, if a veneration for the religion of a people who profess and call themselves Christians, and a fixed resolution to consider a decent respect for Christianity among the best recommendations for the public service, can enable me in any degree to comply with your wishes, it shall be my strenuous endeavor that this sagacious injunction of the two Houses shall not be without effect.

With this great example before me, with the sense and spirit, the faith and honor, the duty and interest, of the same American people pledged to support the Constitution of the United States, I entertain no doubt of its continuance in all its energy, and my mind is prepared without hesitation to lay myself under the most solemn obligations to support it to the utmost of my power.

And may that Being who is supreme over all, the Patron of Order, the Fountain of Justice, and the Protector in all ages of the world of virtuous liberty, continue His blessing upon this nation and its Government and give it all possible success and duration consistent with the ends of His providence.

- John Adams

The Avalon Project. Lillian Goldman Project. Yale Law School

Primary Source Analysis

1. Type of Document: _____

2. Date of Document: _____ 3. Author of Document: _____

4. Title of the Document: _____

5. Who is the Document's Intended Audience: _____
_____
_____
_____

6. List three things the author said that you think are important:_____
_____
_____
_____

7. Why do you think the document was written:
_____
_____
_____

8. What is the evidence that helps you understand why it was written:
_____
_____
_____

9. List two things the document tells you about life in the United States at the time it was written:
_____
_____
_____

10. Write a question to the author that is left unanswered by the document:
_____
_____
_____

My Opinion Piece: John Adams: Inaugural Address

Topic: Based solely on the Inaugural Address of John Adams, summarize your opinion of President Adams' political views.

In my opinion, the political views of President John Adams include: _____

_____

_____

_____

_____

_____

_____

_____

_____

_____

_____

_____

_____

_____

_____

_____

_____

_____

_____

_____

_____

_____

_____

_____

_____

_____

_____

_____

_____

_____

My opinions are backed by the following: _____

_____

_____

_____

_____

_____

_____

_____

_____

_____

_____

_____

_____

_____

_____

_____

_____

_____

_____

_____

_____

_____

_____

_____

_____

_____

_____

_____

_____

_____

_____

John Adams and Thomas Jefferson: Patriots and Adversaries

John Adams and Thomas Jefferson met in 1775 at the First Continental Congress. They were immediate friends who grew to be ardent political adversaries, mostly due to the competitive nature of both men and the extreme political differences they shared. Over a span of fifty years, the men wrote over 380 letters to one another.

At the first Continental Congress, John Adams, Thomas Jefferson, Roger Sherman, Robert Livingston and Benjamin Franklin worked together to write the Declaration of Independence. Jefferson did most of the writing – with advice and edits from the others. Years later, when Jefferson's wife died, the third president of the United States became a regular visitor to the home of John and Abigail Adams.

Both men were foreign diplomats for the young and growing United States of America: Jefferson in Paris and Adams in London. When George Washington was elected President – Adams and Jefferson were pitted against each other for the first time and their political differences became apparent. Jefferson was a Democratic-Republican advocating for limited government and increased State control, while Adams was a devout Federalist who believed in strong centralized power.

The friendship was further taxed, when in 1796, Adams beat, albeit by a narrow margin, Jefferson as Washington's successor for the office of the President. In the next election of 1800, Adams was defeated by Jefferson – but before Jefferson took office – Adams used his power as President to appoint many of Jefferson's political opponents to high ranking positions.

It was not until both men left politics, or as much as a politician can leave politics, did they renew their friendship. This was in 1812. Both men died on the same day – July 4, 1826.

Read the following primary source and complete both the Critical Thinking Questions and the Primary Source Analysis:

Thomas Jefferson to John Adams, December 28, 1796

Below is a letter written by Jefferson to Adams on December 28, 1796, congratulating Adams on being elected president. On James Madison's advice, the letter was never sent. This letter is from <u>The Works of Thomas Jefferson in Twelve Volumes</u>. Federal Edition. Collected and Edited by Paul Leicester Ford.

Monticello, Dec. 28, 1796.

Dear Sir,--The public & the papers have been much occupied lately in placing us in a point of opposition to each other. I trust with confidence that less of it has been felt by ourselves personally. In the retired canton where I am, I learn little of what is passing: pamphlets I see never: papers but a few; and the fewer the happier. Our latest intelligence from Philadelphia at present is of the 16th inst. but tho' at that date your election to the first magistracy seems not to have been known as a fact, yet with me it has never been doubted. I knew it impossible you should lose a vote north of the Delaware, and even if that of Pennsylvania should be against you in the mass, yet that you would get enough South of that to place your succession out of danger. I have never one single moment expected a different issue; & tho' I know I shall not be believed, yet it is not the less true that I have never wished it. My neighbors as my compurgators could aver that fact, because they see my occupations & my attachment to them. Indeed it is impossible that you may be cheated of your succession by a trick worthy the subtlety of your arch-friend of New York who has been able to make of your real friends tools to defeat their and your just wishes. Most probably he will be disappointed as to you; and my inclinations place me out of his reach. I leave to others the sublime delights of riding in the storm, better pleased with sound sleep and a warm birth below, with the society of neighbors, friends & fellow-laborers of the earth, than of spies & sycophants. No one then will congratulate you with purer disinterestedness than myself. The share indeed which I may have had in the late vote, I shall still value highly, as an evidence of the share I have in the esteem of my fellow citizens. But while in this point of view, a few votes less would be little sensible, the difference in the effect of a few more would be very sensible and oppressive to me. I have no ambition to govern men. It is a painful and thankless office. Since the day too on which you signed the treaty of Paris our horizon was never so overcast. I devoutly wish you may be able to shun for us this war by which our agriculture, commerce & credit will be destroyed. If you are, the glory will be all your own; and that your administration may be filled with glory, and happiness to yourself and advantage to us is the sincere wish of one who tho' in the course of our own voyage thro' life, various little incidents have happened or been contrived to separate us, retains still for you the solid esteem of the moments when we were working for our independence, and sentiments of respect & affectionate attachment.

Questions for Analysis

1. Analyze the letter from Jefferson to Adams that was never sent. Discuss what it says about Jefferson's feelings and opinions regarding Adams.

_____

_____

_____

_____

_____

2. Search the internet for the following primary sources. Based on your interpretation of the reading write an argument, support your claims and dispel any counterclaims with relevant evidence. Be sure to clarify the relationships between claims and evidence. For example, use transitions and word choices, such as *furthermore*, *in addition to*, etc. to clarify the relationship between claims and counter claims. (CCSS W. 9 -10.W.1).

Use the template on the following page to help get started as you read through your resources.

---

1. Jefferson to Abigail Adams, Paris, February 2, 1788, in *Papers of Thomas Jefferson**, 12:533.

2. http://www.monticello.org/site/jefferson/john-adams#footnote6_38h0rxe

3. Jefferson to Madison, January 30, 1787, in *Papers of Thomas Jefferson*, 11:96.

4. Adams to Jefferson, March 1, 1787, in *Papers of Thomas Jefferson*, 11:190.

5. Jefferson to Abigail Adams, June 13, 1804, in Cappon, *Adams-Jefferson Letters*, 1:270.

---

*Boyd, Julian P., Charles T. Cullen, John Catanzariti, Barbara B. Oberg, et al, eds. *The Papers of Thomas Jefferson*. Princeton: Princeton University Press, 1950-. 33 vols.

A free online version of this edition is now available from the National Archives through the Founders Online Project: http://founders.archives.gov/about/Jefferson.

Investigating Non-Fiction Texts

Reading and investigating non-fiction for information requires you to stop, question and clarify ideas as you connect points within a text and between texts. Below is a list of questions to help guide your reading. Feel free to ask your own questions as you become more comfortable with this reading strategy.

- What do I understand so far? What do I still need to know?
- What is essential in this paragraph(s)?
- How does this section relate to the reading purpose?
- How do the visuals on the page connect to the titles?
- How does this section connect to the surrounding visuals?
- How does this relate to the chapter thesis or main point of the work?
- What is the purpose of this section?
- How does this information relate to the lecture (or course) concepts?
- How does this section relate to previous sections?

This assignment may be done alone or in groups. If working in groups:

1. Read a designated small portion of the text silently.

2. Select a question. Have members of the group take turns selecting and/or asking questions like those put forth above. One question should be asked for each portion of the text read. It is helpful to break up a one page letter that is not divided into paragraphs into three or four parts.

3. As a group, spend a few minutes answering your questions together. Write everything down in your graphic organizer titled: **Non-Fiction Investigation**.

If completing alone:

1. Read the text.

2. Answer the questions.

"Facts are stubborn things; and whatever may be our wishes, our inclinations, or the dictates of our passions, they cannot alter the state of facts and evidence." John Adams

"A government of laws and not of men." John Adams

"We are in the very midst of a revolution the most complete, unexpected and remarkable of any in the history of nations." John Adams

Text Title: _____

Investigative Question	Your Response
Write your question here and site the paragraph you are questioning. Paragraph No. _____	Record your response here.
Write your question here and site the paragraph you are questioning. Paragraph No. _____	Record your response here.
Write your question here and site the paragraph you are questioning. Paragraph No. _____	Record your response here.
Write your question here and site the paragraph you are questioning. Paragraph No. _____	Record your response here.

Controversy in the White House

John Adams succeeded George Washington as president of the United States in 1797, becoming the first and last Federalist president in U.S. history.

Alexander Hamilton started the Federalist Party during Washington's first term as president and while Washington was sympathetic to the Federalist cause – he did not label himself as such, but rather remained a political independent for the duration of his career. The Federalists worked to build a large group of supporters who believed in a strong national government. The Federalists not only called for a strong centralized system, but for a national bank, tariffs and strong British relations. Their political opponents were the Democratic-Republicans, led by Thomas Jefferson and James Madison, who denounced most of the Federalist policies.

When John Adams took office, the Federalist Party had controlled Congress and the rest of the national government from the beginning of the new nation. Adams and the other Federalists believed that their political party *was* the government. They also believed that once the people had elected their political leaders, they held the power and no one should criticize them. They even passed legislation to those ends, such as the Naturalization Act of 1798.

The Naturalization Act was the first of four pieces of extremely controversial legislation that, together, were known as the Alien and Sedition Acts. These acts strengthened the power of the Federal government under the guise of avoiding a war with France.

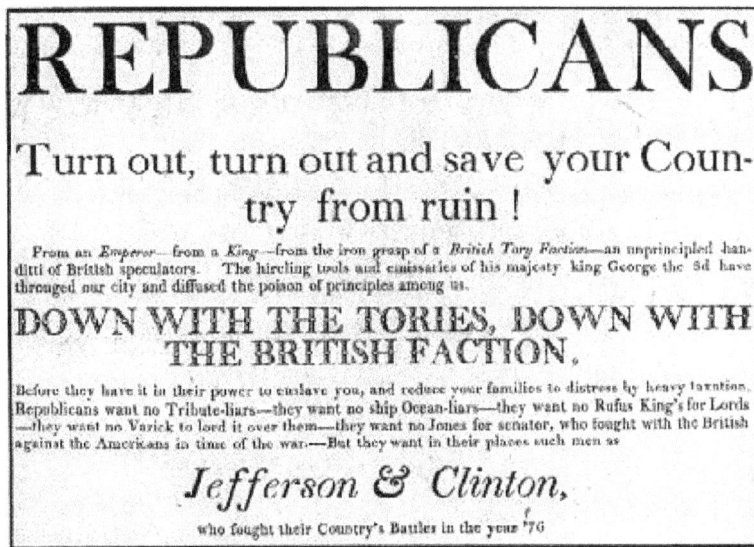

Figure 4: A campaign poster. Library of Congress.

Even thought Adams never enforced the Naturalization Act, he was chastised by the Jefferson led Republicans. The Jefferson Republicans felt the Naturalization Act and the three subsequent acts were unconstitutional and tyrannical. The second act passed was the Alien Act, which gave the president the authority to deport aliens during peacetime. The Alien Enemies Act gave the president the power to deport any alien living in the U.S. who had ties to wartime enemies. Last, the Sedition Act gave the office of the President the power to define what was treason – including any writing that was false or malicious. The Sedition Act was drafted to target any newspaper or pamphlet daring to print anything against Adams during his administration.

The Sedition Act was viewed by most as the most egregious of the four new pieces of legislation as it was believed by some to violate the First Amendment. There was strong anti-Federalist opposition to these acts and this opposition helped Thomas Jefferson win the presidency in 1800.

The Alien and Sedition Acts, 1798

An Act concerning Aliens.

Sec. 1. *Be it enacted by the Senate and House of Representatives of the United States of America in Congress assembled*, That it shall be lawful for the President of the United States at any time during the continnuance of this act, to *order* all such *aliens* as he shall judge dangerous to the peace and safety of the United States, or shall have reasonable grounds to suspect are concerned in any treasonable or secret machinations against the government thereof, to depart out of the territory of the United States, within such time as shall be expressed in such order, which order shall be served on such alien by delivering him a copy thereof, or leaving the same at his usual abode, and returned to the office of the Secretary of State, by the marshal or other person to whom the same shall be directed.

And in case any alien, so ordered to depart, shall be found at large within the United States after the time limited in such order for his departure, and not having obtained a *license* shall not have conformed thereto, every such alien shall, on conviction thereof, be imprisoned for a term not exceeding three years, and shall never after be admitted to become a citizen of the United States.

Provided always, and be it further enacted, that if any alien so ordered to depart shall prove to the satisfaction of the President, by evidence to be taken before such person or persons as the President shall direct, who are for that purpose hereby authorized to administer oaths, that no injury or danger to the United States will arise from suffering such alien to reside therein, the President may grant a *license* to such alien to remain within the United States for such time as he shall judge proper, and at such place as he may designate.

Find and circle the words:

"…combine, conspire, to oppose or impede any law of the United States"

"Intimidate any person holding an office from performing his duty"

"Attempt to procure any insurrection, riot, unlawful assembly"

Put these statements in your own words:

Discuss what type of people would be involved in these activities:

In the 1790s:

Today:

And the president may also require of such alien to enter into a bond to the United States, in such penal sum as he may direct, with one or more sufficient sureties to the satisfaction of the person authorized by the President to take the same, conditioned for the good behavior of such alien during his residence in the United States, and not violating his license, which license the President may revoke, whenever he shall think proper.

Sec. 2. *And be it further enacted*, That it shall be lawful for the President of the United States, whenever he may deem it necessary for the public safety, to order to be removed out of the territory thereof, any alien who may or shall be in prison in pursuance of this act; and to cause to be arrested and sent out of the United States such of those aliens as shall have been ordered to depart therefrom and shall not have obtained a license as aforesaid, in all cases where, in the opinion of the President, the public safety requires a speedy removal.

And if any alien so removed or sent out of the United States by the President shall voluntarily return thereto, unless by permission of the President of the United States, such alien on conviction thereof, shall be imprisoned so long as, in the opinion of the President, the public safety may require.

Sec. 3. *And be it further enacted*, That every master or commander of any ship or vessel which shall come into any port of the United States after the first day of July next, shall immediately on his arrival make report in writing to the collector or other chief officer of the customs of such port, of all aliens, if any, on board his vessel, specifying their names, age, the place of nativity, the country from which they shall have come, the nation to which they belong and owe allegiance, their occupation and a description of their persons, as far as he shall be informed thereof, and on failure, every such master and commander shall forfeit and pay three hundred dollars, for the payment whereof on default of such master or commander, such vessel shall also be holden, and may by such collector or other office of the customs be detained.

And it shall be the duty of such collector or other officer of the customs, forthwith to transmit to the office of the department of state true copies of all such returns.

Sec. 4. *And be it further enacted*, That the circuits and district courts of the United States shall respectively have cognizance of all crimes and offences against this act.

And all marshals and other officers of the United States are required to execute all precepts and orders of the President of the United States issues in pursuance or by virtue of this act.

Sec. 5. *And be it further enacted*, That it shall be lawful for any alien who may be ordered to be removed from the United States, by virtue of this act, to take with him such part of his goods, chattels, or other property, as he may find convenient; and all property left in the United States by any alien, who may be removed, as aforesaid, shall be and remain subject to his order and disposal, in the same manner as if this act had not been passed.

Sec. 6. *And be it further enacted*, That this act shall continue and be in force for and during the term of two years from the passing thereof.

Approved, June 25, 1798.

Amendment I

Congress shall make no law respecting an establishment of religion, or prohibiting the free exercise thereof; or abridging the freedom of speech, or of the press; or the right of the people peaceably to assemble, and to petition the Government for a redress of grievances.

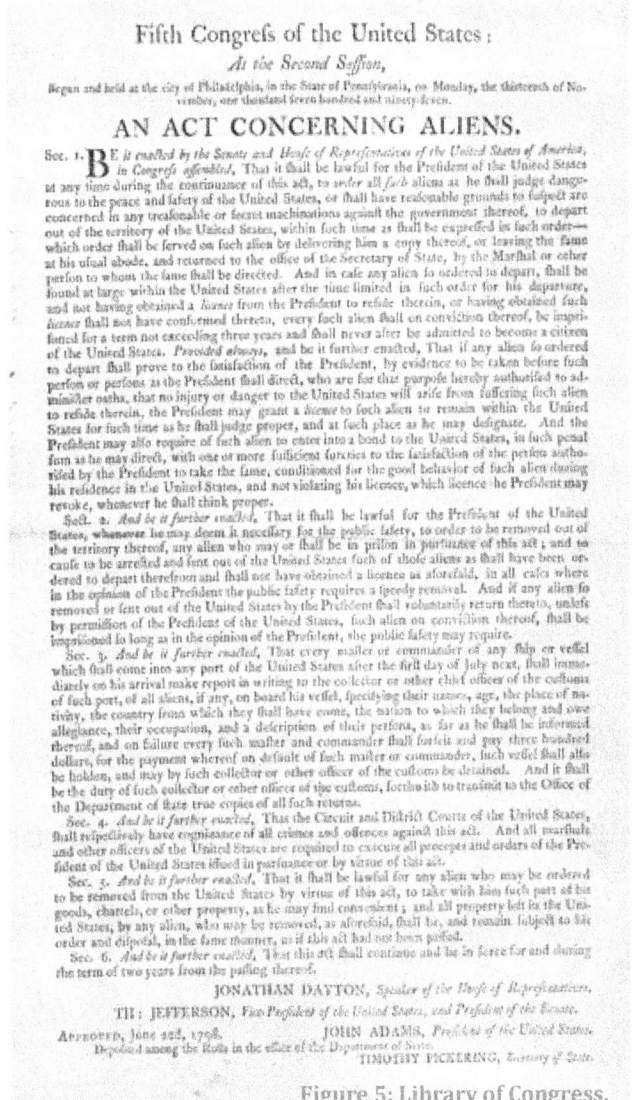

Figure 5: Library of Congress.

Analyze and Synthesize the Alien and Sedition Acts
in Relation to the First Amendment

Assignment 1:

1. Analyze the Alien and Sedition Acts and the First Amendment.
2. Explore the rights and limitations to the concept of free speech.
3. Investigate the impact of American foreign policy on domestic policy.
4. Pose an argument for or against the Alien and Sedition Acts.
5. Explore the counter-argument to your assertion.
6. Support your assertion.

Assignment 2:

Background: During times of war and national crisis there have been other attempts to stifle dissent, including Ex parte Milligan during the Civil War, Schenck v. U.S. (1919) during World War I, the Red Scare in the early 1920's, the Smith Act in 1940, and the Patriot Act after September 11, 2001.

1. Read the Patriot Act at http://epic.org/privacy/terrorism/hr3162.html.
2. Compare and contrast the Patriot Act with the Alien and Sedition Acts.
3. Be prepared to discuss and support your assertions.

Assignment 3:

Research and be prepared to discuss the consequences of the enforcement of the Sedition Act including:

A. The defeat of the Federalists in the election of 1800, and the election of Thomas Jefferson to the presidency.
B. The Kentucky and Virginia Resolutions of 1800 that called for the nullification of the Sedition Act.

Figure 6: A cartoon depicting the political climate with the passing of The Alien and Sedition Acts.

Assignment 1:

Alien and Sedition Acts vs. the First Amendment	
Argument:	
Supporting Statement:	
Supporting Statement:	
Supporting Statement:	
Counter Argument:	
Statement Refuting Counter Claim:	
Statement Refuting Counter Claim:	
Statement Refuting Counter Claim:	
Conclusion:	

The Alien and Sedition Acts vs. The Patriot Act
Compare and Contrast

The Alien and Sedition Acts	Both	The Patriot Act

Primary Source Letter: After not corresponding for eleven years, John Adams wrote to Thomas Jefferson on January 1, 1812. This was the first of many letters that would be exchanged until their deaths on July 4, 1826.

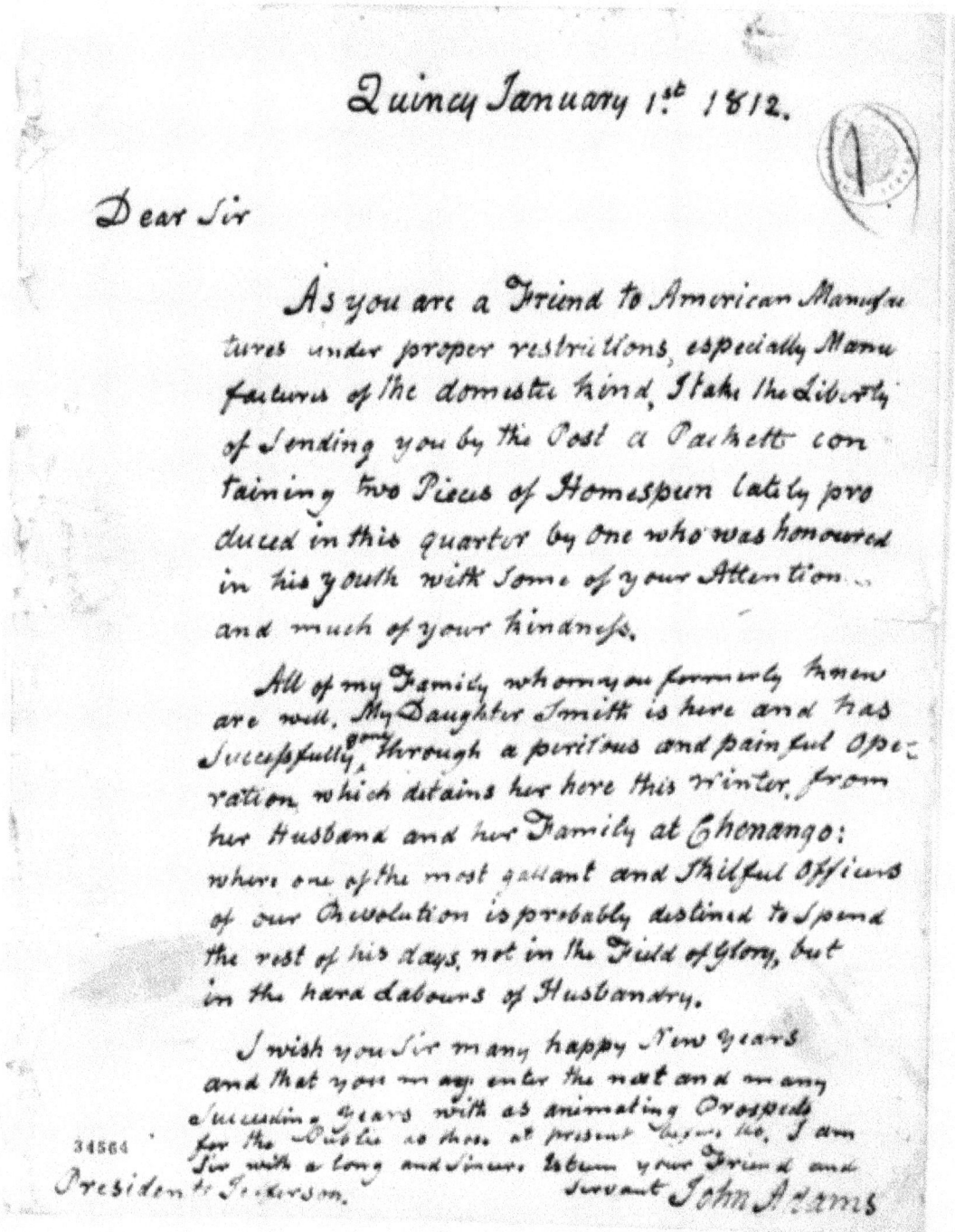

Primary Source Analysis

1. Type of Document: _____

2. Date of Document: _____ 3. Author of Document: _____

4. Title of the Document: _____

5. Who is the Document's Intended Audience: _____
_____
_____
_____

6. List three things the author said that you think are important:_____
_____
_____
_____

7. Why do you think the document was written:
_____
_____
_____

8. What is the evidence that helps you understand why it was written:
_____
_____
_____

9. List two things the document tells you about life in the United States at the time it was written:
_____
_____
_____

10. Write a question to the author that is left unanswered by the document:
_____
_____
_____

Primary Source Analysis: The last letter written by Adams to Jefferson on **April 17, 1826**.

Document Analysis

1. Type of Document: _____

2. Date of Document: _____ 3. Author of Document: _____

4. Title of the Document: _____

5. Who is the Document's Intended Audience: _____
_____
_____
_____

6. List three things the author said that you think are important:_____
_____
_____
_____

7. Why do you think the document was written:
_____
_____
_____

8. What is the evidence that helps you understand why it was written:
_____
_____
_____

9. List two things the document tells you about life in the United States at the time it was written:
_____
_____
_____

10. Write a question to the author that is left unanswered by the document:
_____
_____
_____

Culminating Assignment: John Adams Journal

Imagine you are John Adams, beginning in 1765 and continuing through his presidency in 1800, write a yearly journal entry describing the events of the year including your thoughts, feelings and hopes for the future.

Journal Writing Rubric

	20	15	10	5
Research	Research contains citations, accurate and derived from primary sources.	Research is mostly sited and accurate. Primary source documents are mainly used.	Research contains errors in accuracy and is missing source citations. Or source citations are not reputable.	Little evidence of research. Contains inaccurate information.
Creativity	Posts are creative and believable. You understand John Adams and speak in his voice.	Posts are believable and there is some evidence that you understand who Adams was.	Posts are short and lack creativity.	Posts are incomplete and some are missing.
Conventions	Contains fewer than five errors in conventions.	Contains 6-10 error in conventions.	The patriots may have spelled phonetically and punctuated creatively, but you may not. Contains between 10-20 errors.	Contains more than 20 errors.
Presentation	Contains copies of pictures, letters and other source material, along with most posts (at least 13). The years are scrapbooked (lined notebook paper is fine). Journal is neat and looks polished.	Contains copies of pictures, letters and other source material for at least 10 posts. Journal is neat.	Contains fewer than seven pictures or source material.	Messy or no supplemental source materials included.
Posts	Required number of entries are completed. (35) Volume of writing shows evidence that time and care were put into journal entries.	One to five journal entries are missing. Volume of writing shows evidence that some time and care were put into journal entries.	Six to eight journal entries are missing and/or volume of writing shows not enough time when into project completion.	Nine or more journal entries are missing, and/or volume of writing shows lack of effort.

Resources

- Library of Congress American Memory Collection: http://memory.loc.gov/ammem/index.html
- UC Berkeley Digital Library: http://sunsite.berkeley.edu
- Bancroft Library: http://bancroft.berkeley.edu/collections/
- Early California Population Project (ECPP): http://www.huntington.org/Information/ECPPmain.htm
- New York Public Library Digital Collection: http://digitalgallery.nypl.org/nypldigital/index.cfm
- National Archives and Records Administration: http://www.archives.gov/index.html
- Making of America Project: http://quod.lib.umich.edu/m/moagrp/
- Smithsonian Institution Libraries: Digital Collections: http://library.si.edu/collections/
- Founders Online: http://founders.archives.gov
- Library of Congress: http://www.loc.gov/teachers/usingprimarysources/finding.html
- PBS: The American Experience: http://www.pbs.org/wgbh/amex/adams/filmmore/ps.html
- Colonial Williamsburg Foundation: http://www.history.org
- University of Virginia: http://guides.lib.virginia.edu/content.php?pid=22202&sid=160259
- The Gilder Lehrman Collection: https://www.gilderlehrman.org/collections

For teaching resources email: publisher@luckyjenny.com. Please post "Adams Teaching Resource Request" in the subject line.